aloud in my head

D0993897

For Caz, who had the idea,
pulled back the curtains, and let it appear.

First published 2008 by Walker Books Ltd
87 Vauxhall Walk, London SE11 5HJ

This edition published 2015

2 4 6 8 10 9 7 5 3 1

Preface and anthology © 2008 JonArno Lawson
Individual commentaries © 2008 individual poets
Illustrations © 2008 Jonny Hannah

The rights of the authors of the works comprising this anthology and the right
of Jonny Hannah respectively have been asserted by them in accordance with
the Copyright, Designs and Patents Act 1988

This book has been typeset in M Klang, Sanvito MM and Forte

Printed in Great Britain by Clays Ltd, St Ives plc

All rights reserved. No part of this book may be reproduced, transmitted
or stored in an information retrieval system in any form or by any means,
graphic, electronic or mechanical, including photocopying, taping and
recording, without prior written permission from the publisher.

British Library Cataloguing in Publication Data:
a catalogue record for this book is available from the British Library

ISBN 978-1-4063-6308-1

www.walker.co.uk

aloud in my head

Children's poets discuss a poem each

edited by
JonArno Lawson

illustrated by
Jonny Hannah

Contents

preface

Poems try out poets as much as poets try out poems. As you read through these commentaries you might be surprised by how often an idea, a memory, a word, an image or a rhythm imposed itself on someone, who then was faced with the task of discovering what it meant, or of how to make sense (or nonsense) of it.

Even after a poem has made itself known, it remains puzzling. How does a poem work? No one seems to know, really, but in the commentaries some very interesting insights into the making of certain poems are offered by those who wrote them.

The selection I made was not intended to be exhaustive, or exclusive in any way – it was hard to limit it to twenty-one poems – and I have not attempted to make anything more (or less) than an enticing sampler of great work in a field that's full of exciting and original voices.

From the beginning I had the idea of approaching this in a way that was "inclusively Anglophile" – as Richard Wilbur put it when he saw the proposed list of poets. While the majority are from England and the United States, there are also poets here from Canada, Australia, Guyana, India, Scotland, New Zealand, Ireland and

South Africa. You may notice, as a point of interest, that what rhymes in one accent doesn't necessarily rhyme in another. "Diva" and "beaver", for instance, might rhyme in England, but in North America the hard "r" at the end of "beaver" might, for some, ruin the rhyme's effect.

I selected poems that surprised me. It seems like an embarrassment of riches to have them collected all together in one book. The poets were also asked to explain something about how they came to be. For some reason I expected more overlap in the commentaries, and I was delighted when they came back as varied and fascinating and unalike as the poems they were discussing.

I can't emphasize enough how important it is to read the poems out loud. I don't think you'll be able to appreciate them fully until they've entered your mind through your ears as well as your eyes.

There's so much more I'd like to say about the book, but I'll stop here and let the poems (and poets) speak for themselves.

JonArno Lawson

John Agard

Poem and Commentary

Old World New World

Spices and gold once cast a spell
On bearded men in caravels.

New World New World cried history
Old World Old World sighed every tree.

But Indian tribes long long ago
Had sailed this archipelago.

They who were used to flutes of bone
Translated talk of wind on stone.

Yet their feathered tongues were drowned
When Discovery beat its drum.

New World New World – spices and gold
Old World Old World – the legends told.

New World New World cried history
Old World Old World sighed every tree.

Commentary

To mark the beginning of the new century in the year 2000, there was an anthology of poems I had great pleasure in editing. It was entitled *Hello New* and a number of poets were invited to contribute a new poem. It was a very open-ended invitation. The poets were free to go down any road as long as the word "new" appeared in the poem.

The results were exciting and intriguing: from the welcome of a newborn lamb or moving into a new house to dipping into a new book or having to come to grips with a new language. The variety of subject and approach by the poets showed how one little word can be a springboard into a poem, and it also gave the reader that thrill of encountering the word "new" in an unexpected context. That was the challenge and the fun.

And that was also the background to the inspiration for **"Old World New World"**, which first appeared in that anthology. I was hoping to use "new" in a not too predictable way. I suppose poets are always hoping to inject the familiar with freshness and surprise. As one poet, Ezra Pound, famously put it: "Poetry is news that stays news."

So thinking about the word "new" led me to thinking

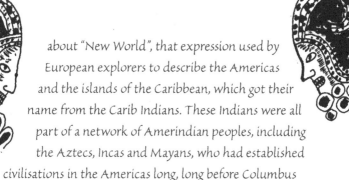

about "New World", that expression used by European explorers to describe the Americas and the islands of the Caribbean, which got their name from the Carib Indians. These Indians were all part of a network of Amerindian peoples, including the Aztecs, Incas and Mayans, who had established civilisations in the Americas long, long before Columbus was even born. To these "pre-Columbian" peoples, whose canoes were sailing the Caribbean many centuries before Columbus' ships, the lands were not exactly new, but to the sixteenth-century Europeans, they were an "undiscovered" world – a New World.

When I was at school in Guyana, where I was born and grew up, there was never any mention that the Vikings and the Phoenicians might also have sailed to the Americas. Our history books always said that the history of the West Indies began with the arrival of Columbus, ignoring the indigenous peoples who had long inhabited the region. In the Guyana rainforest, for example, there are living descendants of ancient Amerindian tribes such as the Carib and the Arawak. You could say their presence is a reminder of old pre-Columbian civilisations. Do they bear witness to an Old World or a New World?

All this, of course, might make interesting history, but interesting history doesn't necessarily make interesting poetry. The poem seeks to invoke the shadow behind the facts and to invite the words not just to relate but to resonate, hopefully in a concise and memorably musical way.

"**Old World New World**" brings together in one breath a meeting of two worlds, two civilisations, two hemispheres. One of those hemispheres had bows and arrows and no horses. The other had guns and horses. The Amerindian civilisation, as you know, was to be destroyed in what is called the age of conquest or the Age of Discovery.

But you don't want to overload your poem with too much information, like a room cluttered with furniture. You want to leave space for the reader's imagination to feel at home. Sometimes two rhyming words can bounce off each other like atoms and chime a thought into being. Take **"caravels"** and **"spell"**. The word **"caravels"** (light, fast-sailing ships developed by the Portuguese) has a somewhat threatening sound. Columbus and his men arrived in a fleet of **"caravels"**, driven by the desire for gold and exotic spices as if they were under some kind of spell.

For the Amerindian peoples, the so-called New World was rich in ancient myth. For them, the feathers from tropical birds like the macaw and hummingbird were a natural part of their dress as well as something to exchange at the market and on the battlefield. Feathers were also used in medicine and as offerings to the gods. Feathers were companions in rituals and ceremonies.

Why not try reading the poem aloud? Poems get excited when they're read aloud. Yes, try out your **"feathered tongues"**. And I'll keep my fingers crossed that you will no longer be a reader curled up in an armchair, but a wise old shaman or shawoman offering up a few words on the fate of two worlds (**"Old World New World"**) and how they will affect each other forever.

John Agard

Carol Ann Duffy

POEM
AND
COMMENTARY

Five Girls

Philomena Cooney
wears green sandals,
yellow ribbons,
silver bangles;
knows three secrets,
lives in a tent
in the middle of a field
near the River Trent.

Arabella Murkhi
speaks in Latin
keeps her cat in,
sleeps in satin.
Went to Turkey
just like that.
Absolutely *loved* it.
Amo amas amat.

Isadora Dooley
loves her jewellery.
Pearls on Sundays,
diamonds Mondays,
rubies Tuesdays,
Wednesdays blue days,
Thursday Friday Saturdays
It-doesn't-really-matter days.

Esther Feaver,
opera diva
dressed in beaver,
loved a weaver;
took a breather,
grabbed a cleaver,
now the weaver
will not leave her.

Joan Stone
liked a good moan,
lived on her own
in a mobile home.
The doorbell never rang,
neither did the phone;
so she pressed her ear
to the dialling tone.

Commentary

I wrote this poem to amuse my daughter,
Ella, when she was four or five. Two of the
names are the names of real children she
knew at the time. One is a name recalled
from my own childhood – **"Philomena"**
always sounded strange and exotic to me.
I liked following the rhymes for each name.

My own mother invented similar
rhymes to amuse me when I was a child.
The other great influence on me in
childhood was the work of Lewis Carroll.

Carol Ann Duffy

16

dodgson

Aquarium

Fishes swim
without a goal
in aquarium or bowl.
We can watch them
through the glass:
bits of sunshine as they pass
in a circle round and round...
Little fish are nowhere bound.
They don't know
the mighty motion
of the waves and
of the ocean.
They must wait
for time to pass
locked up in a cage of glass.

Commentary

I am a South African writer who started writing very late in life and since 1984 have published about twenty-five books, mostly nonsense verse. In 1996 I was asked by a South African music organisation to write poems to accompany Saint-Saëns' "Carnival of the Animals" (1886). A year after completing a version in Afrikaans, I decided to write English words. I chose not to translate the Afrikaans poems directly, but to have each poem completely new. Here is the Afrikaans poem with a literal line-by-line translation:

AKWARIUM

Vissies glip
en vissies gly–
'n reënboog
voor my oë verby.
Vissies swem
en vissies plas–
hoef hul lywe
nooit te was;
eet nooit boontjies
eet nooit kool;
gaan ook nimmer
na 'n skool.
Ek bly hier
en hulle dáár
en nooit sal ons
kan saambaljaar
Vissies swem
en vissies plas,
maar tussen ons
–'n muur van glas

AQUARIUM

Fishes slip
and fishes glide–
a rainbow
before my eyes.
Fishes swim
and fishes splash–
and never need
to wash their bodies.
They never eat beans
nor cabbage;
they never need to
go to school.
I remain here
and they remain there
and we will never
romp together.
Fishes swim
and fishes splash
but between us
–a wall of glass.

After so many years, I cannot remember how the English poem was written. But I did find some scraps of sentences in a notebook, one of many I sometimes grab when I need a clean piece of paper (the same notebook contains notes, addresses and even recipes I jotted down between 1984 and 2006):

> Fish all swim without a goal
> in the silence of a bowl
>
> You don't know the sea and ocean
> You don't feel the mighty motion
>
> divided by a wall of glass

To me the discovery of these jottings shows the truth of A. A. Milne's words: "One of the advantages of being disorderly is that one is constantly making exciting discoveries!" It also proves that the poem was not written in one sitting.

I remember seeing a cartoon of two fish swimming in a goldfish bowl and the baby fish asking the mother: "Are we there yet?" This suggested to me the swimming without an end in sight.

Because Saint-Saëns' piece of music is known as **"Aquarium"**, my phrase "in the silence of a bowl" was later changed to **"in aquarium or bowl"**. I think **"a cage of glass"** is much better than "a wall of glass", as it emphasizes the idea of being imprisoned.

Looking back, I've also noticed a few things that were intuitively written into the poem, such as the many "s" and "sh" sounds, which suggest the sound of water splashing – **swim, glass, bits, fishes, watch, sunshine, motion**.

But I prefer not to analyse my own poems, and when people read things into my work that I myself did not specifically intend, I start believing that maybe I am cleverer than I thought!

Philip de Vos

Jackie Kay

The Stincher

When I was three, I told a lie.
To this day that lie is a worry.

Some lies are too big to swallow;
some lies so gigantic they grow

in the dark, ballooning and blossoming;
some lies tell lies and flower,

hyacinths; some develop extra tongues,
purple and thick. This lie went wrong.

I told my parents my brother drowned.
I watched my mother chase my brother's name,

saw her comb the banks with her fingers
down by the river Stincher.

I chucked a stone into the deep brown water,
drowned it in laughter; my father puffing,

found my brother's fishing reel and stool
down by the river Stincher.

I believed in the word disaster.
Lies make things happen, swell, seed, swarm.

Years from that away-from-home lie,
I don't know why I made my brother die.

I shrug my shoulders, when asked, raise my
eyebrows: *I don't know, right, I was three.*

Now I'm thirty-three. That day they rushed me
to the family friends' where my brother sat

undrowned, not frothing at the mouth, sat
innocent, quiet, watching the colourful TV.

Outside, the big mouth of the river Stincher
pursed its lips, sulked and ran away.

Commentary

What makes us remember what we remember? What things, when we look back, stick out in clear colour? I was interested in guilt and memory in this poem. We often remember very clearly – horribly clearly – times in our lives when we have let ourselves down, or done things we regret or embarrassed ourselves. This poem is about a lie I told when I was three. I still don't know why I did it. But I remember it so vividly because I felt guilty about it for years.

The images of lies flowering and growing extra tongues, of lies ballooning and blossoming, are an attempt to capture the ripple effect of guilt. Guilt grows in dark closets and multiplies. In childhood, things loom very large; you can stay awake worrying about something very small. In childhood, things quickly get out of proportion. **"Lies make things happen, swell, seed, swarm."** *I used the alliteration here so that the reader continues with that "ssss" sound, snake sound. There's a contrast in the poem between the nightmarish, swarming world of the lie, and the innocent, slightly boring world of the truth. My brother sits* **"undrowned, not frothing at the mouth … "**, *watching TV. It's all very ordinary. The imagination is wild! The imagination is a wild beast!*

There's also the idea in the poem of the river enjoying a story being told about itself, as if the river had encouraged the girl to lie, or had some part in it. I liked the idea of trying to show how we can wriggle out of taking responsibility for what we say; how quickly we turn around and say, "It wasn't me," or "He made me do it."

The other thing I was trying to capture was the great exhilaration and hysteria involved in telling something totally outlandish. **"Drowned it in laughter"** – there is a lovely freedom to be found in making things up! Now I write all the time; and in some way writing and lying, making a fiction out of some truths, walking the borderline between truth and fiction, is my bread and butter. I am still walking the banks of the river as a writer.

The Stincher is a river in the south of Scotland near Ballantrae. The incident actually happened by a river near Drymen called the Erskine. But I loved the name Stincher better because it sounded like an onomatopoeic word for lie. I could imagine someone saying, "She told a right Stincher," meaning she told a whopper! In poems you can change the names of rivers and never get accused of lying. That's what I like about writing poems. I can make things up quite legitimately.

Jackie Kay

27

X. J. Kennedy
POEM AND COMMENTARY

Iguana

Iguana demonstrates the signs
  Of somewhat hasty wrapping:
Beneath its chin a fold of skin
  Hangs downward, loosely flapping.

The quiet victim men forget
  In desert bomb-test sectors;
In Hollywood the pampered pet
  Of horror-film directors

Who need a live iguanadon –
  Oh, then Iguana's happy
To glue a few fake backfins on
  And play its great-grandpappy.

Commentary

The little poem **"Iguana"** came about in what was,
for me, an unusual way. A publisher had suggested an
alphabetical book of poems for kids, with each poem
dealing with a different animal, bird, or insect, arranged
from A to Z. I don't usually take on jobs that aren't my
own idea, but somehow the notion was irresistible.
Eventually the result was a book called **Did Adam Name
the Vinegarroon?** The vinegarroon is a kind of scorpion
that, when you bother it, gives off the smell of pickles.
(Honest, there IS such a creature!)

I started out with Archeopteryx for the letter "A" –
that's a long-ago flying lizard, a prehistoric ancestor of our
robins and sparrows. But certain letters of the alphabet
resisted. They didn't immediately suggest any subjects. Oh
oh, I groaned to myself – this job is going to be like pulling
teeth. At first the letter "I" seemed one of those hard ones.
So I got out my dictionary and began reading through all
the words that began with I, looking for animals. There
was IBEX, IBIS, but I didn't know what to say about those.
Then I came to a picture of an IGUANA, and a light bulb
in my head started flashing. Iguanas, to my surprise, were
something I cared about.

And why was that? Back when I was twelve years old, I

had been greatly impressed by a movie called *One Million B.C.* It wasn't at all historically accurate, for it showed cavemen and dinosaurs living at the same time, but it was a slam-bang rouser of a movie. In one scene, a caveman played by actor Victor Mature waved a spear, holding off a giant iguanadon that was doing its best to gobble up actress Carole Landis, playing a cavewoman with long blonde hair who looked as if she had just stepped out of a beauty shop. Oh boy, I thought, what a thrilling movie. Still, I couldn't help wondering. How in the world had they managed to find a real live dinosaur and bring it to Hollywood?

Then a newspaper story about the movie made it all clear. The film-makers had taken an ordinary iguana, which has spiny projections on its back, and had pasted fins onto them, making the little beast look like its **"great-grandpappy"** the iguanadon, that dinosaur of similar name. Then, as it waddled along, the camera zoomed in on it and made it look enormous.

In fact, that iguana wouldn't have been the least bit interested in devouring Carole Landis. It would have preferred a nice juicy fly.

Later on, another news report had struck me, haunted me, stayed in my memory. When atomic bomb tests were conducted in New Mexico, some lizards had been blown up along with the bomb. Had they been some poor, innocent iguanas who happened to live on the test site? I didn't know for sure, but reckoned they might have been.

All of that miscellaneous information was material for a poem. I started scribbling lines. It has been so many years since then that to tell you the truth I don't remember much about the actual writing of the poem. It probably had to be worked over and revised a few times. Most poems do, even if at first they quickly emerge in rough form. I wish I could get things right the first time, but that practically never happens, so I just keep writing and writing and trying to get a poem right, and filling up my wastebasket.

X. J. Kennedy

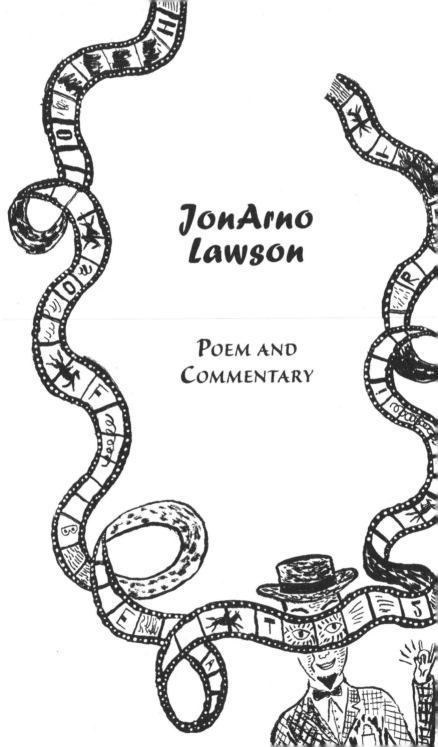

JonArno Lawson

POEM AND COMMENTARY

The Octopus and the Seahorse

The seahorse bowed to the octopus
and asked if she would please
join him in his night-time dance
around the coral keys.
Her shyness put his aquatic
quasi-equestrian heart at ease.
She blinked her eyes and then she bowed,
bending her many knees.

They danced, they danced –
the Octopus-Seahorse dance –
in their many-legged
multi-coloured barnacle-covered pants.
They danced, they danced –
and their twirling was much enhanced
by the current above the seabed floor
and their oceanic trance.

Commentary

Few poets know why they've written a poem until after they've written it, and even then it isn't always clear. But usually it's possible to figure out where certain ideas and images in the poem come from.

HOW FEELINGS SOMETIMES TURN INTO ANIMALS

The octopus and the seahorse are both shy, gentle sea animals. They are also hard to categorize – what is an octopus exactly? And what is a seahorse? Is it a fish? I often find it hard to say who or what I am as well. I'm also shy, and like to think I'm gentle. In other words it's very possible that I thought of the octopus and the seahorse because they reminded me of myself in some way.

HOOFBEATS FIRST

Very often, the rhythm of a poem comes before the poem itself. I sometimes find myself tapping with my fingers before I think of a single word I'm going to write. It's a bit like hearing hoofbeats before you can see the horse or the rider.

THE MYSTERIOUS MIGRATIONS OF MEMORIES

When I was eight years old, I moved briefly to Miami, Florida. Though I spent only a few months there over thirty years ago, I remember it as if it were yesterday. I have clear memories of the surprising sea creatures I watched from the shore, or found washed up on the beach. Many of these creatures, over the years, have crept out of my memories and into my poems.

A STRIKING IMAGE

The seahorse is very small; the octopus is, comparatively, very large; this creates a comic element to their attraction. It also makes for a striking image (I think so, anyway). At the same time, it's touching that they're not concerned about their obvious difference in size, and that they're being so formal with, and considerate to, each other.

IF THE POEM HAS MOVEMENT AND STRIKING IMAGES, IT WILL, WITH A BIT OF IMAGINATION, RUN LIKE A SHORT MOVIE IN YOUR MIND

In this poem there is constant movement. The two creatures are very formal and almost cautious at the beginning, but by the end they've let themselves go completely. When I think of this poem it runs through my mind like a small movie: the seahorse bows, the octopus blinks, they begin their dance – a whirling dance – and, as they whirl about the coral, even the current adds something to their dancing. Either from the whirling or from happiness, or from both, they go into a trance, and this adds something to the dance too – they're not self-conscious anymore. Their movements have become free.

ARE THOUGHTS THE PLAYTHINGS OF WORDS OR WORDS THE PLAYTHINGS OF THOUGHTS?

As far as the writing of the poem goes, I was proudest of the ridiculous phrase **"aquatic quasi-equestrian"**. It was the hardest, and at the same time the most fun part of the poem to write. The "kw" sound is not a common one in English, and to find three "kw" words that would run together naturally while still making sense (and at the same time sounding like comical nonsense) wasn't easy.

When I first wrote the poem, I had it nearly all done on the first go, aside from those difficult fifth and sixth lines (**"Her shyness put his aquatic/quasi-equestrian heart at ease"**); I had no idea what to put there. I left it blank. Then, after a few weeks, I put in "Her hesitating shyness put his equestrian heart at ease" – I was on the right track when I came up with the word "equestrian", which means "relating to horse-riding", but the line was dull. So I kept thinking about it, on and off, and finally it occurred to me that **"aquatic"** would work well. And then, as I was trying to figure out a new line with **"aquatic"**, the word **"quasi"** popped into my head, and I had it.

I couldn't believe my luck: I knew what **"quasi"** meant, but I couldn't suppress a superstitious impulse to double-check it in the dictionary.

Once I start looking at a poem from many different angles, dozens of different associations crop up, and it's difficult to know which were relevant to the making of the poem, and which are associations or memories triggered or unearthed by the poem after it was made. Trying to figure out how a poem works (or doesn't) is every bit as entertaining as writing it, I think. It's just as easy to slip into the realm of nonsense, and, simultaneously, to make unexpected discoveries.

JonArno Lawson

Dennis Lee

Poem
and
Commentary

Alligator Pie

Alligator pie, alligator pie,
If I don't get some I think I'm gonna die.
Give away the green grass, give away the sky,
But don't give away my alligator pie.

Alligator stew, alligator stew,
If I don't get some I don't know what I'll do.
Give away my furry hat, give away my shoe,
But don't give away my alligator stew.

Alligator soup, alligator soup,
If I don't get some I think I'm gonna droop.
Give away my hockey-stick, give away my hoop,
But don't give away my alligator soup.

Commentary

One day I didn't go to the store, and I came back with alligator pie. And then I went to the store.

It's true. It was 1966, and I had two young daughters. And since my wife and I loved Mother Goose, we were reading lots of nursery rhymes at bedtime. After a while I started making up rhymes of my own. The old rhymes are wonderful, I thought, but why not have some new ones too?

On this particular day, I had to go buy something or other at the store. I got on my bike, and I headed off down our street in central Toronto. But after about twenty seconds, something interrupted me.

My legs were going round and round as I pedalled, and there was a particular rhythm when my left foot, and then my right, pressed the pedal down. I began to hear snatches of words that echoed the rhythm: *"All-i-ga-tor pie ... All-i-ga-tor pie"* ... Da *dum*-da, da *dum*-da ... I *think* I'm gonna *cry* (sigh? die?)...

I had no idea where this had come from. The words were ridiculous, and I wished they'd go away; I had to buy the something-or-other, after all, and I wanted to get home and get back to my writing. But more of these nutty words were arriving: *Give* away the (*dump*-itty-dum) ... Give away the (fly? sky? eye?) ... **"But don't give away my ... alligator pie."**

The wretched thing wouldn't stop – now I was hearing **alligator stew** too. Eventually I couldn't keep all the words in my head. So in exasperation I turned the bike round, rode back home, and scribbled down as much as I could remember: a couple of verses, with lots of holes. Thank goodness I got rid of that, I thought. Then I rode to the store, bought the something-or-other, and that was the end of that.

Except there was a little more. I finished the poem later on, and I read it to my daughters and other kids, and it turned out that whenever a child heard it, she couldn't forget it. So it went into my first children's book, and in fact it became the title poem. And now there are kids all round the world who chant that rhyme, and most of them have never heard of Dennis Lee.

Which is fine by me. I'm just glad I didn't keep going to buy the something-or-other.

Dennis Lee

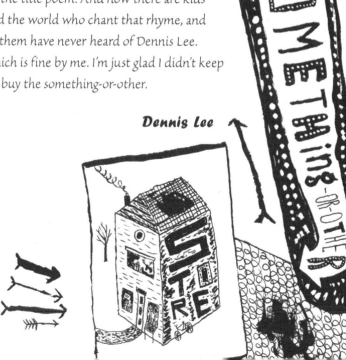

Margaret Mahy

POEM AND COMMENTARY

The Man from the Land of Fandango

The man from the land of Fandango
Is coming to pay you a call,
With his tricolour jacket and polka-dot tie
And his calico trousers as blue as the sky
And a hat with a tassel and all.
And he bingles and bangles and bounces,
He's a bird! He's a bell! He's a ball!

The man from the land of Fandango
Is coming to pay you a call.
Oh, whenever they dance in Fandango
The bears and the bison join in.
And the baboons with bassoons make a musical sound,
And the kangaroos come with a hop and a bound,
And the dinosaurs join in the din.
And they tingle and tongle and tangle
Till tomorrow turns into today.
Then they stop for a break and a drink and a cake
In their friendly fandandical way.
The man from the land of Fandango
Is given to dancing and dreams.
He comes in at the door like a somersault star
And he juggles with junkets and jam in a jar
And custards and caramel creams.
And he jingles and jongles and jangles
As he dances on ceilings and walls,
And he appears every five hundred years
So you'd better be home when he calls.

Commentary

Sometimes it is hard for a poet to say exactly
where poems come from. Poems sometimes
tell stories or they pass some wonderful picture
into your mind – something beautiful, something funny.
A lot of the poems that I manage to write are to do with
the sound of words. When I read them afterwards, I
think, "There are jokes with the sound of words hidden in
these lines". I write the poems down on a page, but I like
to think that some reader somewhere will actually say the
poem aloud. It would mean that the poem is set free from
the page and will be heard out in the open air.

There are many moments of amazement in life. On an
ordinary day we may see something that takes us by
surprise; something as simple as a spring flower, or a
cat creeping along the top of a wall. This morning I saw
four birds flying across the sky in a certain formation – I

couldn't tell if they were ducks or wild geese. I was filled
with an unexpected astonishment. I forgot all the things
I was supposed to be doing and stood staring up at them.
And of course there are other astonishing moments
when something really remarkable is taking place, when
some wonderful gymnast is turning somersaults and
cartwheels, or a clown suddenly appears in a
supermarket and juggles balls, making jokes as he (or
she) juggles. **"The Man from the Land of Fandango"** is
about a moment like that. Of course, the poem is partly
a joke about astonishment, but I think it might also have
something mysterious about it hidden in the words. And
I like to think that, as you read the poem or say the poem
or hear the poem, colourful pictures will fill your head.
You will actually see the Man from Fandango juggling
custards and caramel creams.

Writing this poem I imagined people living an ordinary life, but then, suddenly, everything changes around them. The Man from the Land of Fandango – from the land of the imagination – leaps into the room like a somersault star. Everyone can see him as he twists and turns and juggles.

Of course, moments of astonishment come much more frequently than every five hundred years. That is a joke in the poem. In real life, astonishment and wonder can leap in on you at any moment. You do need to be at home in your own head when they call, however. Once I had the idea for this poem, once I had the image of that bounding man of Fandango in my head, I don't think it took me long to write it. It just seemed to bounce along out of the end of my pen.

When I had it written down on paper, I began to make changes. I liked the idea of using words beginning with the same letter because I thought alliteration would make the words a little bit tongue-twister-ish, fun to say aloud or to hear secretly in your head as you read the poem: **"And he bingles and bangles and bounces/He's a bird! He's a bell! He's a ball!"** As I write poems down I always read them aloud to myself just to see how they sound in the outside air.

Margaret Mahy

Adrian Mitchell

POEM
AND
COMMENTARY

Riding West from Little Bear

I ride a horse called Secrets
A lively dapple-grey
His hoofbeats echo down the trail
They call the Milky Way

Past a stampede of meteors
Down the ravines of space
And over the deserts of silver dust
Watchfully we pace

We journey on with hopeful hearts
Though the way's long and far
But sometimes halt and light a fire
Upon some lonesome star.

Commentary

When I was a child I was given two globes.
One was the wonderful usual kind, with all the countries
of the world trying to squash into the seven continents,
many of them coloured pinkish-red to indicate they were
supposed to belong to the king of England. But the other
globe was very dark and blue all over, sprinkled with
white circles and dots which represented the planets and
stars and galaxies. And there was our planet Earth, in the
middle of the Milky Way. And I was out there too, with
my mother and father and my brother Jimmy and my two
globes. By day I lived on the Earth globe, but by night I
dreamed on the dark blue sky globe. So space has always
seemed like home to me. I love the sun and stars and
planets and meteors and especially our gentle moon.

For most of my life I have been half in love with America.
It started with American jazz, which was my rebel music
when I was a teenager. I was excited by American comics
and then by American poets like Walt Whitman and
Theodore Roethke and Kenneth Patchen and Allen
Ginsberg. Most of the movies I saw were American.

I never saw the USA until I was twenty-two, and
then I took a train ride right across it, from New York
to Seattle. I was enchanted by the incredible variety of

landscapes and climates – and by the friendliness of the people. I've been back many times, though nowadays my feelings about the USA are very mixed, because of the stupid and cruel wars conducted by the American government.

But even before I heard jazz, my brother and I were given cowboy suits. Our cowboy trousers had sheepskin chaps down the front of the legs. My brother's chaps were white, like everyone else's. But mine were black wool. At first I was unhappy about this, but somehow my lovely mother persuaded me that they were very stylish.

That was a thousand years ago, but still I sometimes play cowboy in my daydreams. I jump off a train in a strange city and mutter under my breath, "I've come to clean up this town." But I've really only come to perform my poems.

As a child I used to ride an enormous German ex-cavalry horse called Baroness. One day she stopped suddenly on a steep hill, but I kept going over her head and woke up in bed. It stopped me riding, but I still admire horses.

"Riding West from Little Bear" started as a poem about riding over a desert. I climbed on the horse and decided that he was called **"Secrets"** – which is one of my favourite words. It's a word like a parcel that I want to unwrap and find what's in it. **"Dapple-grey"** is another special word for me, for the sound of it and its rhyme with Apple Day.

I was riding across a rocky landscape towards a ramshackle Western town called Little Bear. But then I realized that it wasn't a town I was headed for, it was the Little Bear itself, the famous star, child of the Great Bear. So we must be riding through space. But I hung on to Western words like **"trail"** and **"stampede"**, **"ravines"** and **"lonesome"**. Then I saw that the trail underneath the hooves of Secrets was the Milky Way itself. And then

I saw the meteors stampeding and said: "Slow down, Secrets. I want to take it all in." It was beautiful out there in space, I felt free and easy. But I kept watch just in case of any trouble.

The poem doesn't have an end. It just pauses, on some lonesome star. I light a fire to cook a meal and warm us overnight. I feed and water Secrets. I say to him: "You know what? I don't mind if this journey goes on for ever."

What's the point of going on? To find some kind of peace. Maybe when we reach the Little Bear.

Adrian Mitchell

Adrian Mitchell asks that none of his poems be used in exams or tests.

Roger McGough

POEM
AND
COMMENTARY

Didgeridoo

Catfish
take catnaps on seabeds
Sticklebacks
stick like glue
Terrapins
are terrific with needles
But what does a didgery do?

Bloodhounds
play good rounds of poker
Chihuahuas
do nothing but chew
Poodles
make puddles to paddle in
But what does a didgery do?

A puffin
will stuff in a muffin
A canary
can nearly canoe
Hummingbirds
hum something rotten
But what does a didgery do?

Tapeworms
play tapes while out jogging
Flies
feed for free at the zoo
Headlice
use headlights at night-time
But what does a didgery do?

What does a didgery
What does a didgery
What does a didgery do?

Commentary

A didgeridoo is a musical instrument made from eucalyptus wood or bamboo pipe, invented by native Australians, which not only makes a lovely dark sound but has a fine name.

Kedgeree is a popular breakfast dish of lightly curried rice, smoked fish and hard-boiled eggs, originating from India. The poem started life as a joke I scribbled in one of the little notebooks I always carry with me:

What is fishy, eggy and plays music at breakfast?

A Kedgeree doo

I had obviously been thinking about the word didgeridoo, because next to that scribble I had written:

But what does a didgery Do.

And having asked myself that question, I had to answer it. But not right away.

Several weeks later, in another notebook, a larger one that I keep on my desk, I sat down to answer the question, and the poem took wing once I imagined the didgery as an animal.

The next step was to assemble a list of other creatures whose names I could play with.

"Terrapins" for instance suggested "pins and needles" and **"terrific"** uses the first four letters of "terrapin" too. Sticklebacks sticking, chihuahuas chewing, hummingbirds humming; I bet you could make up a completely different list to create your own version of the poem.

From the outset, I realised that I needed to find words to rhyme with "do" and this wasn't difficult, but a more interesting challenge was to find unusual "internal" rhymes that would amuse the reader and keep the poem on its toes: **"Bloodhounds /good rounds"**, **"Puffin/ stuff in/muffin"**, **"Canary/can nearly"**, **"Headlice/ headlights"**.

My proudest moment came when the poem was performed on children's television by a man who also played the didgeridoo.

Roger McGough

Stephen Mitchell

POEM AND COMMENTARY

The Wishing Bone

It happened on a winter's day
(The air was cold, the sky was grey):
Out walking in the woods alone,
I came upon a wishing bone.

I picked it up and wished the sky
As warm and gentle as July.
I wished sweet music in the air
And flowers growing everywhere.

I wished an apple orchard and
A beach with sugar-flavoured sand,
A lake, a little birch canoe.
And everything I wished came true.

I wished down tinier than a flea,
Wished up above the tallest tree,
I wished me as a wolf, a shark,
A firefly shining in the dark,

A blade of grass, an ocean wave,
A bear asleep inside its cave.
I wished a talking daffodil.
I wished a dragon I could kill.

I wished a flock of purple geese.
I wished the world eternal peace.
I wished a pair of angel's wings.
And then a thousand other things.

But after many days had past,
Each wish seemed easier than the last,
And I felt bored as stiff as stone,
And wished the wishing off the bone.

And suddenly I stood at ease
Among the bare and patient trees
One ordinary winter's day.
The air was cold. The sky was grey.

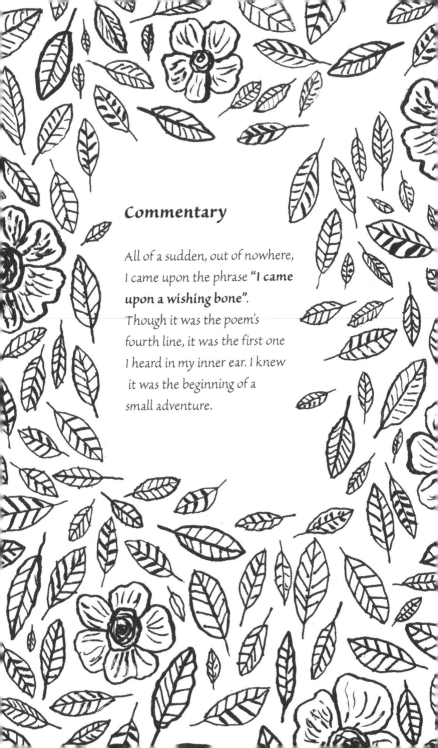

Commentary

All of a sudden, out of nowhere,
I came upon the phrase **"I came
upon a wishing bone"**.
Though it was the poem's
fourth line, it was the first one
I heard in my inner ear. I knew
it was the beginning of a
small adventure.

I was sitting at my desk in a garage in
Berkeley, California. It was winter, and the
garage was impossible to heat, so I would wear
a down coat, stick my legs into a sleeping bag,
slip on a pair of fingerless gloves, and settle
down to work.

I was as intrigued to discover my line
as the narrator of the poem must have been
to make *his* discovery. Actually, the whole poem was
contained in that one line. I knew that it would be about
finding and getting beyond magic. It would also be about
the four-beat iambic couplet, one of the simplest verse
forms in the English language. The challenge would be how
to vary the rhythms from stanza to stanza so that they
would always be slightly different and always seem fresh.

The first three lines wrote themselves quickly. It **was** a
winter's day; the air **was** cold. After **"alone"** conveniently
appeared, to rhyme with **"bone"**, I thought, *Hmm. Where
is it going to go from here?*

Well, of course, summer: that was easy enough. The
child who was the speaker of the poem (I imagined him as
being six years old) started with three obvious wishes: not
only summer and flowers, but **"sweet music"** (the phrase
had an Elizabethan feeling to it). Then he wished an apple
orchard, which I hadn't expected. But the bigger surprise

was that the line rhymed on "and".
That was interesting; up to this point
the rhymes had been fairly conventional.

I liked it that there was a surprise in every line. **"Sugar-flavoured sand"**, for example. The wishes expanded as my little narrator began to test the limits of wishes. And the poem was still just twelve lines old.

The challenge here was to suggest a whole universe of wish-fulfilment within a few stanzas. The narrator turned out to be a junior Walt Whitman: he becomes everything he can think of, from the vast to the tiny, from the dangerous to the heroic. I particularly liked the line **"I wished the world eternal peace"**. This comes close to the essence of what most people think of as prayer, and though it's a compassionate desire, there's a hugely egotistic thought behind it: *If I were God, I could do a better job with the world.*

How would the poem conclude? I knew that the narrator would have to see that "My will be done" is a dead end, that ultimately happiness can come only from the deep acceptance of reality expressed in "Thy will be done." How could I convey that in a couple of stanzas?

It all unfolded naturally in the wake of the word **"But"**. I liked the expression **"I felt bored as stiff as stone,"** because it brought to life the cliché "bored stiff".

The next line startled me a bit. There was a brave finality to the boy's decision, with no chance for second thoughts. What is the world like when you've let go of control – of whatever control you thought you had? You get to live in a truth that even the dearest wish can't hold a candle to.

The last stanza has a Zen simplicity to it. The key words are **at ease**. When what you want is what you have, of course you're at ease. What is special about this state of ease is the "nothing special" of it. And I particularly liked that these lines grouped themselves three by one, rather than two by two. That delighted my ear as much as the meaning delighted my mind.

Stephen Mitchell

Grace Nichols

POEM AND COMMENTARY

Sun is Laughing

This morning she got up
On the happy side of the bed,
Pulled back
The grey sky-curtains
And poked her head
Through the blue window
Of heaven.

Her yellow laughter
Spilling over,
Falling broad across the grass,
Brightening the washing line,
Giving more shine
To the back of a ladybug
And buttering up all the world.

Then, without any warning,
As if she was suddenly bored,
Or just got sulky
Because she could hear no one
Giving praise
To her shining ways,
Sun slammed the sky-window closed,
Plunging the whole world
Into greyness once more.

O Sun, moody one,
How can we live
Without the holiday of your face?

Commentary

The changeability of the English weather always keeps me on my toes, and in a way was the inspiration for the poem. Since living in England (for the past thirty years) I've developed much more of a "weather-eye". In Guyana, where I grew up, we take the sun for granted. No one says, "What a glorious day." We only tend to comment on the weather when it's raining.

Living in England has changed all that. I am much more aware of what's happening outside, and the weather is a hot topic of conversation in our home, whether we're moaning, with an exaggerated shiver, at someone who's left the front door open in winter or using the sun as an excuse to go out: "It's going to be wet and cold tomorrow. Better make the most of it."

On a nice sunny day it's difficult to get me to stay at home. It was one such day that triggered the poem. I was in high spirits as I could see the sun beckoning me to come and bathe in its glow. I got dressed quickly – I knew things can change rapidly. But by the time I was ready, much to my disappointment, it was dark and grey again. It was as if someone had switched off a light in the sky or closed a window, blotting out the sun.

So at one level you could say that **"Sun is Laughing"** is about the feel-good effect that the sun has on me. At a wider level, it's a slightly playful homage. Even though the different English seasons have their own magic (I love the colours of autumn) I still miss the amazing yellowness of the sunlight back in the Caribbean.

The poem was written fairly quickly. It came at one sitting. I have to work much more at some of my other poems. I think the reason for this is that the sun has always figured strongly in my imagination and I'd been collecting my impressions for a long time, without consciously thinking about it. That morning, the sight of the sun suddenly going in disappointed my "weather-eye" but triggered the joy of a poem. I saw sun as a temperamental teenage girl going off in a huff to her room (my apologies to teenage girls, but I do have two daughters of my own).

I hardly made any changes to the poem once I'd written it. In the beginning I thought of Sun getting up on the "right side of bed" as a sign that she was in a good mood. We speak of someone getting out of the "wrong side of bed" when they wake up in a bad mood. In the end, I chose **"happy side of the bed"**. Happy seemed right.

I like reading this particular poem. The way it unfolds down the page in a simple narrative, telling a little story. I particularly like the ending –

> O Sun, moody one,
> How can we live
> Without the holiday of your face?

because I hadn't thought of the line **"the holiday of your face"** until I had actually written it. Interestingly, the word "holiday" comes from the words "holy day."

In the act of writing a poem, ideas and feelings and images link up in surprising ways. You might ask why I made the sun female when the moon is usually seen as female. Well, in many cultures, including in some of our own Amerindian folk stories, the sun is seen as a goddess figure with a glittering mirror and this is what might have prompted me to make Sun in the poem a young woman.

Grace Nichols

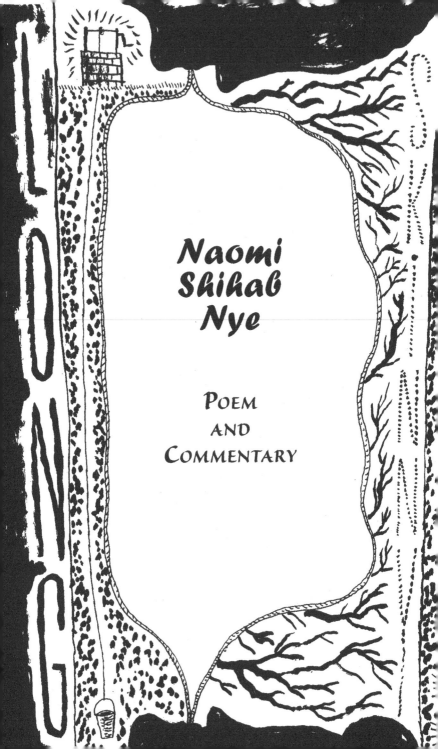

Supple Cord

My brother, in his small white bed,
held one end.
I tugged the other
to signal I was still awake.
We could have spoken,
could have sung
to one another.
We were in the same room
for five years,
but the soft cord
with its little frayed ends
connected us
in the dark,
gave comfort
even if we had been bickering
all day.
When he fell asleep first
and his end of the cord
dropped to the floor,
I missed him terribly,
though I could hear his even breath
and we had such long and separate lives
ahead.

Commentary

A few years ago, I was spending the night in an old inn in Michigan, when I found myself staring at a satiny, braided white cord with fringes, holding back the curtain. Ping! Another similar cord I hadn't thought of for many years popped back into my brain.

The first cord used to function as a "telephone line" between my brother's bed and mine, in our childhood home in St Louis. I don't know where we got it. We didn't "talk" on it – we just tugged it back and forth. Different cord, different state, whole different era, but – something felt connected again. An image linked to another image. At that moment, I really missed my brother.

I love the way connections can click together and link up unexpectedly. Something you did not realize was still living in the deep well of your brain rises to the surface and shines again.

THE SHAPE

Since the poem was about a cord, it needed to be long and skinny.

Writing a poem is always an experiment.

Which words do you choose, what shape do the lines take? The more you write, the more you feel mysterious little instincts humming inside the words. I like a poem that takes you into the scene right away. I hope a reader can easily "see" the cord stretching between the brother and sister in the two twin beds on either side of the room.

Rituals between people who know each other well can be comforting. I wanted the poem to suggest that we held onto the cord's two ends many nights in our early lives, and we liked it. It was our quiet little tradition. When my mother read this poem, about 45 years later, she said, "What cord?"

When I was about 11, our parents turned the garage into another bedroom and moved me out there. I hated it. Not only was I scared of the mice and bugs who might find me in the place the washing machine and car used to live, there was no cord long enough to reach my brother on the other side of the house. This information is not in the poem. But I thought of it while writing. I have always been interested in what we do not include when we write a poem. Every written poem has another silent, unspoken world around it.

MEMORY RISING

I had not thought of the fact my brother always fell asleep first for many years. But when I saw the cord in Michigan, that memory rose too. I'd feel so lonely when he disappeared into dreamland and I worried about the

shadowy branches outside our bedroom window. I also
worried about the closet, and what might be happening
inside it while we slept. I was afraid the spiders were
building colonies in there.

THE SOUNDS

The poem is full of "s's" and "c's" – the two initial letters in
the title. That might be just a coincidence, but "s" is also
the first letter of "sleep" and many "s's" recurring in a poem
create the hissing tide of sleep washing up on two kids
in bed who don't really want to go to sleep yet. Sounds
repeating inside a poem create their own texture.

THE SLIGHTLY MYSTERIOUS ENDING

I'm completely intrigued by how two people who grow up
in the same family can turn out to be entirely different.
My brother and I, as adults, have very little in common.
Our attitudes and ideas on most things – politics, hobbies,
pleasures, travels – are perfectly opposite. We are probably
as different as two people could be. He eats only meat,
I eat only vegetables. He lives in a huge new house, I live
in a tiny old cottage. We have trouble communicating
in words now. We get mad or irritated easily, though
"communication" is a central part of both our jobs.

So I will always miss the brief period of time when

we felt close to one another and shared a room and two ends of the same cord, and wanted to be connected, even though it would feel much harder later on. Falling asleep at different times was just the beginning of a lifetime of differences.

I think poems always help us to look at what we are connected to, and disconnected from. I could not live without them.

Naomi Shihab Nye

Jack Prelutsky

POEM AND COMMENTARY

The Kraken

Deep beneath the foaming billows
something's suddenly amiss
as a creature wakes from slumber
in the bottomless abyss.
And a panic fills the ocean,
every fish in frenzy flees,
for the kraken has awakened
at the bottom of the seas.

It rises to the surface
with an overwhelming noise
and it hunts for mighty vessels
which it crushes and destroys.
Then it chokes a great leviathan
with one stupendous squeeze –
oh the kraken has awakened
at the bottom of the seas.

How it lashes, how it thrashes,
how it flashes, how it flails,
how it dwarfs the greatest fishes,
even dwarfs the mighty whales!
Nothing living in the ocean
can enjoy a moment's ease,
for the kraken has awakened
at the bottom of the seas.

Commentary

In the early 1970s, I was doing summer workshops for children at a public library in Cambridge, Massachusetts. I'd had about ten books of my poetry for children published, and was thinking about what to write next. All of my books until then had been humorous, and I felt that I was getting into a rut. I asked the children's librarian what sort of poetry she thought her young readers would most enjoy. She immediately came up with two topics – monsters and dinosaurs. As soon as she said that, I knew she was right. I decided to tackle monsters first.

I thought back to my days as a not-so-well-behaved little boy who generally declined to obey his mother. For example, when I was about four or five years old, my mother would notice that I ate everything on my plate but the vegetables. "Eat your vegetables," she'd say. "No!" I'd reply. Her voice would get very soft, and she'd practically whisper, "Eat your vegetables, or the bogeyman's going to get you." Without further complaint, I immediately ate all my vegetables.

When I began work on my monster book, which eventually became *Nightmares*, subtitled "Poems To Trouble

Your Sleep", the first poem I wrote was "The Bogeyman", because that was the creature I most remembered from my own childhood. Then I continued with poems about other beings from traditional, well-known folklore, such as vampires, witches, wizards, ogres and trolls. The book was beautifully illustrated with pen and ink drawings by Arnold Lobel, and was an immediate success. I called my editor and proposed doing a sequel.

She readily agreed, and I set to work.

This time I had to do a bit more research than I'd done for *Nightmares*, since some of the creatures I intended to write about were relatively unfamiliar to me. These included the banshee, the poltergeist, the abominable snowman, and the kraken.

I read extensively on the kraken, and was fascinated by sailors' tales of this mammoth sea monster dragging ships to their doom. Sometimes the kraken was described as a giant octopus, sometimes as a monstrous whale, and occasionally as a colossal crab. In all cases, it was an undeniably fearsome creature.

I also loved the sound of the word kraken, and used it as an internal rhyme in the poem: hence, the kraken has awakened. When I recorded the book, *The Headless Horseman Rides Tonight*, in which the poem appears, I emphasized the **"kraken has awakened"** rhyme.

I learned years later that I'd made a fundamental error – I'd never verified the pronunciation of kraken. I'd assumed that the word rhymed with waken – after all, it certainly looked as if it did – but I was wrong. It's actually pronounced "CROCK-in". Recently I've checked every online dictionary, and to my chagrin, have found that kraken is always pronounced "CROCK-in", never "CRAY-kin".

If I had done my homework and checked its pronunciation when I wrote the poem over thirty years ago, I wouldn't have written **"The Kraken"** the way I did. I suspect that the poem I might have written wouldn't be as good as this one – of course, there's no telling. Anyhow, now you must read, "the CROCK-in has awakened". It's really not so bad, and I'm starting to get used to it.

Jack Prelutsky

Anushka Ravishankar

Poem and Commentary

Excuse Me, is this India?

I hopped into a three-wheeled car
And called out "Take me there!"
The driver started off at once,
He never asked me "Where?"

Suddenly he stopped and said,
"At last we're getting near."
"Near to what?" I asked him.
He bellowed in my ear:
"Near to this is far from that!
I think that's very clear!"

Though it wasn't clear to me,
I nodded very cleverly.

At a shop I stopped to see
If I could get a hint
Of where I was, but all I saw
Were clothes of every tint.

"Where am I and what's this place?"
I asked of everyone.
A woman came and said to me,
"You're as far as you can run.
But if you learn to fly, then you
Could catch up with the sun."

I left the shop
With a happy hop.

I hopped until the airport
And there! There was a sign.
But suddenly I realized
I couldn't read a line.

I asked a bearded gentleman.
He said, "Oh don't you know?
It doesn't matter where you are
But where you want to go."

I sat down there
And scratched my head,
And thought of what
The man had said.

Commentary

This excerpt is from a book called *Excuse Me, Is This India?* The illustrator, Anita Leutwiler, is a textile artist who lives in Germany. When she came to India, she collected bits and pieces of colourful cloth, and used them to make quilted pictures of things she had seen – cows on the beach, bandicoots in the garden and three-wheeled cars called autorickshaws.

I looked at the pictures, and wrote a story in verse about a child who turns into a blue mouse and sets off on a fantastic journey to a strange place, where the most unlikely things happen. When I started writing it, though, I wasn't very sure what it was going to be about. All I knew was that it was about a mouse who goes on a journey. Sometimes things just happen as you write, and it's difficult to explain how. That kind of writing is fun; it's like playing. You kick the words around, not getting too worked up about whether they're going in the right direction. Sometimes they don't, and you tear them up and start again. Sometimes they do, and to your surprise and delight you have a poem!

Usually, a book is written first, and then an illustrator creates pictures to go with the words. But this book happened the other way round. When you look carefully at a picture, lots of ideas start shooting off in different directions in your head. The difficult part is weaving all these images and ideas neatly into a story that you want to tell. And when you're writing the story in verse, there's another complication, which should not be taken lightly – the lines have to rhyme! Trying to do this without sounding silly, killing grammar or changing spelling (which I often feel like doing) has turned many a writer bald. There have been times when I've gone through the alphabet – at, bat, brat, cat, chat, drat, doormat – right up to z, and not found a word that would fit. When that happens, you either decide to give up writing and take a job licking envelopes in the post office, or you cunningly change the previous line and end it with a word for which you can easily find a rhyme.

But there are also times when the right word floats into your head a moment before you write it, and who can tell where it came from? It happens rarely. Most of the time writing is a lot of sweating and hair-pulling and ink-splattering.

In the poem, the journey of the blue mouse has the unreal, random feel of a dream, where events need not make sense at all. The blue mouse goes from place to place asking the cow, the bandicoots, the elephant and the humans she meets the same question in different ways: **"Where am I?"** Each of them gives her an outrageous, nonsensical answer, which baffles her even more.

The verse in this book is mostly nonsense verse, which is a special kind of verse. It seems to make sense, but if you read it carefully, you realize it's quite absurd, and means nothing. For example, the woman in the shop tells the blue mouse: **"But if you learn to fly, then you/ Could catch up with the sun."**

The blue mouse is perfectly satisfied with this answer and leaves the shop with a happy hop. But in fact those lines are nonsensical, as is most of this poem. It may not teach you much about India, but it might leave you hopping happily.

Anushka Ravishankar

Christopher Reid

POEM AND COMMENTARY

Skip Don't Trip

Skip don't trip
the rope's a whip

goes round and round
dabs the ground

a regular beat
for lively feet

to cross with a quick
shuffle a flick

or whisk of the heel
at times you feel

the rope miss
by a whisper a kiss

but don't stop now
it won't allow

the least lapse
suddenly slaps

the ground to make
quite sure you're awake

will dance to its tune
all afternoon

its whip whoop
its swish and swoop

its whizz and clip
its skip skip skip

Commentary

"Skip Don't Trip" is from *All Sorts*, my first book for
children. Many of the poems in it are about children, too.
This one is placed next to a sort of sonnet that describes a
pair of boys sharing a skateboard: one has a leg in plaster and
is pushing the board along with his crutch, while his friend
stands behind as a passenger. I saw this sight one day, near
where I live, and because I admired both the cleverness and
the daring of it – and they were managing it very gracefully
– I wanted to put it into verse. **"Skip Don't Trip"** is about
another, more frequently seen playground activity: skipping.

Because skipping is so common, we tend to take it
for granted, scarcely bothering to stop and look if we don't
happen to be actively involved. But it is an amazing thing,
difficult to do and exciting to watch when it is done with
flair. Many of the different rhymes and chants that go with
it are worth listening to as well.

I suppose when I began my poem, what I should most
have liked was to produce an actual skipping rhyme, for
use in the playground, but that would have been less easy
– impossible, really. The point about such rhymes is that
children themselves have made them up. They belong to
children alone and, unlike poems in books, have not been
supplied by adults or given the questionable blessing of

adult approval. They are
often as lively as they are just
because they are rough and rude,
and this makes them both fun to chant and a
stimulating accompaniment to the serious business of not
letting your feet get tangled in a fast-moving rope that will
show no mercy if you put a foot wrong.

Although I knew I couldn't write a proper skipping
rhyme, I soon saw that I could write something like it:
a poem that might encourage the reader's mind to skip
acrobatically. The most obvious oddity of **"Skip Don't
Trip"** is its lack of punctuation. Punctuation marks make
pauses – but a skipping-rope won't stop for even the
shortest rest, so punctuation had to go, leaving the reader
to pick up the beat by ear alone. The rhymes and line-
breaks are there to help, and by reading the poem several
times it should be possible to catch the beat and reach
the end without getting in a tangle. In actual skipping,
the rhythm of the rope and the movement of the feet
must be timed slightly differently – what musicians call
"syncopation". Making this work needs practice, whether
in jazz, in skipping, or in a poem like this one, which may
look difficult at first sight, but can be managed if you keep
at it. The reward should be the pleasure of feeling your
mind dance a little more nimbly than you thought it was
able to.

Christopher Reid

Michael Rosen

Poem
and
Commentary

Thirty-Two Laps

One Tuesday when I was about
Ten
I swam thirty-two laps
Which is one mile.
And when I climbed out of the water
I felt like a big, fat lump of jelly
And my legs were like rubber
And there was this huge man
There
With tremendous muscles all
Over him
And I went up to him and said
"I've just swum a mile."
And he said,
"How many laps was that then?"
"Thirty-two," I said.
And the man said,
"I've got a lad here who can do ninety."

Commentary

"Thirty-Two Laps" is the true story of what happened when
I swam a mile at what used to be called Harrow Swimming
Baths, not far from Harrow-on-the-Hill underground station.
I spent a lot of time there when I was around ten years old
but I didn't belong to their swimming club. Sometimes people
who run sports clubs at places where the public can go get
quite irritated if a kid from outside does as well as one of
their kids. I guess that's what was going on here.

This extra fact has got absolutely nothing whatsoever to
do with the poem but you heard it here first: I was born just
round the corner from the baths.

Sometimes people ask me why I write poems that don't
rhyme, that seem to sound like short paragraphs, or even
short speeches.

The answer is that when I was young, the poems I
liked were quite often ones that didn't rhyme, that
sounded like speech, or like a stream of thought. One writer
who wrote like this was Dylan Thomas in his play **Under
Milk Wood**, and another was the American poet, Carl
Sandburg, who wrote poems that sounded like
someone talking onto the page.

When I started writing, that was the sound
that I tried to imitate. And as I got older I

found out that many poets had written like
this for over a hundred years – particularly
in France, Germany and America.

It's a way of writing that helps me get to what I
think is the real truth of a moment or a scene from my life.
I can explore it for what really happened and how I feel
about what happened by trying to capture what people
were saying, what I could see and what I could hear.

People have sometimes said to me that this is an
unusual way of writing for children. Well, if it's unusual,
then I say three cheers for that.

If you want to sell millions of books, the best thing
to do is to write in a way that's "usual", or very familiar. I
always think that the best way to write for anyone, children
included, is to write in ways that are UNfamiliar, in ways
that make people surprised or curious. One of the jobs of
a writer is to make familiar things unfamiliar and to make
unfamiliar things familiar. That's what I always try to do.

I realize that this annoys some people. It makes them
very irritated, because they say that what I write "isn't
poetry". Well, I just say, call it something else, then. Don't
worry about what it's called. Call it "stuff" or "thingies" or
"pieces" and put it on one side, rather as the zoologists had
to do when they first saw the duck-billed platypus.

Actually, come to think of it, why not call what I write
"duck-billed platypus"?

Michael Rosen

Jeanne Steig

Poem
and
Commentary

Bellicose Brigand
vs Belligerent Bear

A bear and a brigand were bickering bitterly
Under the shade of a baobab tree.
"The best thing by far," bawled the brigand, "is baklava."
"Bosh!" boomed the bear. "It can't possibly be."

"Why, there's bric-a-brac, ipecac, blubber, and broccoli,
Bamboo, banana oil, beetles, and brine."
"You bandy-legged brute," brayed the brigand, "you
blatherskite!
Baklava beats them all any old time."

Oh what a brouhaha: "Baklava! Balderdash!
Bah!" barked the bear. "We shall never agree."
"Let us pause," breathed the brigand, "and banish this
blabber with hot buttered bat bread and barnacle tea."

Commentary

The question is, Why do I write?
Ah, well, the page, you see, is white,

And I've a thing or two to say.
They're dumb? I'll write them anyway.

I write because I love each word,
I love them more when they're absurd.

The cock-a-mamey ones that jig,
The ones that zag, the ones that zig:

Like flim-flam, hanky-panky, and
Mish-mash or nit-wit – both are grand.

Some words are soft and sneaky, too:
Lumbago, kibosh, ooze, kazoo.

Rambunctious words are pure delight,
There's yuk-a-puck, there's fly-by-night,

They rattle in my head until
I turn them loose. They're rather shrill.

Why do I write? I write because
there is a hunger there that gnaws.

It's like a sort of crazy itch
That stretches to a fever-pitch,

I need to scratch – what else will do?
Not dollar bills, not cheese fondue,

Not fancy boots, not love, not crime:
I've got to sit me down and rhyme.

There is the subject. That will come.
And rhythm, like an echoing drum,

And there are rules one has to keep,
The way musicians bloop and bleep

While keeping time, so they can play
In any hog-wild, tomfool way,

And no ill-wisher dares to state
It makes his blood coagulate

To hear such ring-tailed, roistering notes,
The bleating of a gang of goats.

I'll bet you figured I'd forgot
The reader. No, no, I have not.

For what's the good of writing if
It can't be shared? T'would bore me stiff.

I do love words. And, as I've said,
I write in order to be read.

Jeanne Steig

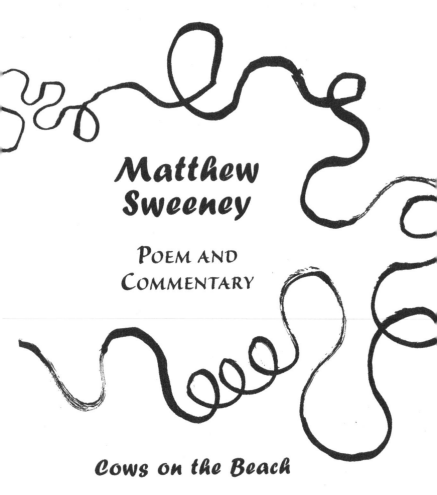

Matthew Sweeney

POEM AND COMMENTARY

Cows on the Beach

Two cows,
fed-up with grass, field, farmer,
barged through barbed wire
and found the beach.
Each mooed to each:
This is a better place to be,
a stretch of sand next to the sea,
this is the place for me.

And they stayed there all day,
strayed this way, that way,
over to rocks,
past discarded socks,
ignoring the few people they met
(it wasn't high season yet).
They dipped hooves in the sea,
got wet up to the knee,
they swallowed pebbles and sand,
found them a bit bland,
washed them down with sea-water,
decided they really ought to
rest for an hour.

Both were sure
they'd never leave here.
Imagine, they'd lived so near
and never knew!
With a swapped moo
they sank into sleep,
woke to the yellow jeep
of the farmer
revving there,
feet from the incoming sea.
This is no place for cows to be,
he shouted, and slapped them
with seaweed, all the way home.

Commentary

What I remember about the writing of **"Cows on the Beach"** is this: I was back in Donegal, where I come from, staying in a house close to the sea. One day I decided to take a walk down there. There were no people on the beach, but right at the water's edge two cows were stepping through the little waves. I was so surprised by this that I ran back to the house to get the camera – at that time the *Observer* newspaper was offering £100 for an unusual photograph, and I was sure the next £100 would be mine. When I got there I realised that my wife had gone off in the car and taken the camera with her, so I had to make do with putting the cows in a poem instead.

I started by asking questions, as I usually do when beginning a poem. How often had they visited the beach? Did they like it there? What did the farmer think of them being there? Very quickly I decided the poem had to be from the cows' perspective, even though I wanted to keep it in the third person – and there had to be a bit of cow-speak in it (whenever I read the poem aloud to young children, I say those lines in a mooey way). I felt this was one poem that had to rhyme, but there had to be a flexibility about the lineation – sometimes long

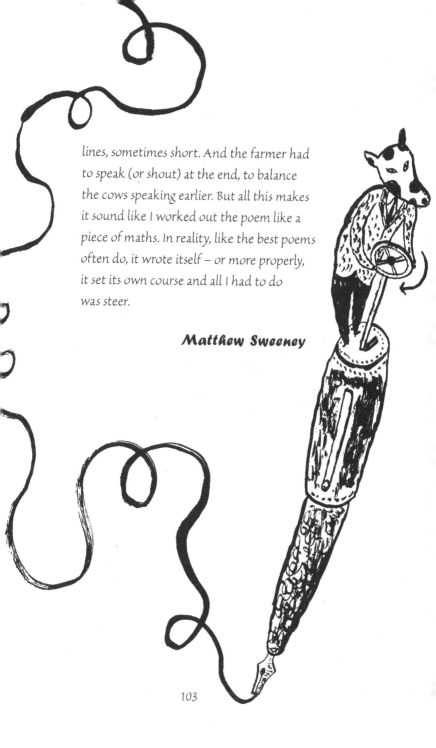

lines, sometimes short. And the farmer had to speak (or shout) at the end, to balance the cows speaking earlier. But all this makes it sound like I worked out the poem like a piece of maths. In reality, like the best poems often do, it wrote itself – or more properly, it set its own course and all I had to do was steer.

Matthew Sweeney

Richard Wilbur

POEM
AND
COMMENTARY

The Disappearing Alphabet

Without the letter I, there'd be
No word for your IDENTITY,
And so you'd find it very tough
To tell yourself from other stuff.
Sometimes, perhaps, you'd think yourself
A jam jar on the pantry shelf.
Sometimes, perhaps, you'd make
   a ticking sound
And slowly move your hands around.
Sometimes you'd lie down like a rug,
Expecting to be vacuumed. Ugh!
Surely my friends, you now see why
We need to keep the letter I.

Commentary

Children are often logical and literate; certainly mine were, and when they were growing up I delighted with them in the logic and illogic of Lear and Carroll, and in all sorts of games with words. When I took to writing my several books for children, I wrote out of that family experience and a home-grown sense of what might amuse a child. With my children in mind, I did two little books of poems and drawings, one called *Opposites* and the other called *More Opposites*.

Sometimes, as in this example, the "opposites" poems were plausible as to what's opposed to what: "What is the opposite of riot?/It's lots of people keeping quiet."

At other times, the attempt to force the world into neat antitheses was arbitrary and absurd. The poems appealed, I think, both to the children's desire for order and to their taste for a measure of honest chaos.

Another book of mine, *The Pig in the Spigot*, consisted of little poems which strove to explain, in some far-fetched manner, why – for instance – we find the word "hick" inside the word "chicken".

It's seldom that you see a hen or cock
Come strolling down a busy city block.
They much prefer the country for their part,
Because a *chicken* is a *hick* at heart.

And here is another small specimen from that book:

> Moms weep when children don't do as they say.
> That's why there is a *sob* in *disobey*.

When I began to write poems for a sequel to that book, I found myself publishing groups of them in grown-up magazines like the *Atlantic Monthly*, under the title "Words Inside of Words: for Children and Others". All of my children's books have, in fact, sought to be the sort of thing which can be enjoyed by adults and children, together or apart. It made me happy to learn, a few years ago, that a woman whom I esteemed kept a copy of *Opposites* in her bathroom.

"The Disappearing Alphabet" is based on the notion that words are our key to reality and that the loss of any letter would cause some part of reality to escape us. Looking now at my lines about the letter "I", I can imagine a nightmarish children's book editor who would say that **"identity"** is too hard a word for young children. I have never met such an editor, but I believe they exist, depriving children of variety and challenge.

Richard Wilbur

Nancy Willard

POEM AND COMMENTARY

Blake Leads a Walk on the Milky Way

He gave silver shoes to the rabbit
and golden gloves to the cat
and emerald boots to the tiger and me
and boots of iron to the rat.

He inquired, "Is everyone ready?
The night is uncommonly cold.
We'll start on our journey as children,
but I fear we will finish it old."

He hurried us to the horizon
where morning and evening meet.
The slippery stars went skipping
under our hapless feet.

"I'm terribly cold," said the rabbit.
"My paws are becoming quite blue,
and what will become of my right thumb
while you admire the view?"

"The stars," said the cat, "are abundant
and falling on every side.
Let them carry us back to our comforts.
Let us take the stars for a ride."

"I shall garland my room," said the tiger,
"with a few of these emerald lights."
"I shall give up sleeping forever," I said.
"I shall never part day from night."

The rat was sullen. He grumbled
he ought to have stayed in his bed.
"What's gathered by fools in heaven
will never endure," he said.

Blake gave silver stars to the rabbit
and golden stars to the cat
and emerald stars to the tiger and me
but a handful of dirt to the rat.

Commentary

Conversation between the Poem and its Author

The Poem: Dear author, though we know each other very well, there are a few questions I have always wanted to ask you.

The Author: Ask away. I also have a few questions I've always wanted to ask you.

The Poem: Fair enough. What gave you the idea of writing me?

The Author: Now that's a good question. Before I answer let me remind you that you are only one of sixteen poems in a book called *A Visit to William Blake's Inn*. The poems in that book will show you what it's like to spend a few days at an inn run by the poet William Blake. You arrive, you meet new friends. Mr Blake enjoys taking his guests out on walks through the neighbourhood, and one of his favourite walks is the Milky Way.

It also happens to be one of mine, though of course I can only walk it in my imagination, and that's one reason I wrote the poem. In the poem I describe the sky as chilly and bright with stars. That is how the sky always looks to me on a clear night. There are two kinds of guests who take this walk: those who love to go star-gathering (rather like gathering seashells) and those who complain about the cold. To help you see and hear the characters taking this walk, I let them speak for themselves. I have always loved dialogue, both in stories and poems.

The Poem: Blake gave such lovely gifts to the rabbit and the cat and the tiger—

The Author: Ah yes, **"silver shoes"** and **"silver stars"**, **"golden gloves"** and **"golden stars"**, and **"emerald boots"** and **"emerald stars"**.

The Poem: But to the rat he gave boots of iron—

The Author: Boots of iron are very practical. So is the rat. He's a bit grumpy, isn't he? He would rather be comfortably curled up in bed than go out exploring on the Milky Way. And for this reason the stars do not look beautiful to him at all. It's the light in ourselves that helps us to see beauty in others. And now, my dear poem, I want to ask you a question.

The Poem: Ask away.

The Author: Why did you want to rhyme? When you popped into my head, I heard the music in you before I even knew the words. It's just as if you were on the other side of the water—

The Poem: What water?

The Author: When you are rowing on a lake, you can

hear voices from a great way off. You can't see who is speaking but you can almost hear what they are saying. That's what you sounded like before I could hear the words.

The Poem: You have answered your own question. I could say that I arrived in rhyme because it is easier to remember poems that rhyme than those that don't and I do want to be remembered. But that's not the whole story. Mr Blake wrote poems that rhymed, and since I'm bringing news of William Blake's Inn, I want to convey it in a way that might have pleased him.

The Author: You know, when I wrote those rhymed lines, I tried to write in a language that is no different from the language we speak every day. I wanted both the words and the order of the words to sound natural, as if speaking in rhyme were the most natural thing in the world. Of course that didn't happen in the first draft. You, my dear poem, went through numerous revisions. It took a lot of revisions to make you sound as if I hadn't laboured over you at all.

The Poem: Would you have written me differently if I had not been one of sixteen poems about the inn?

The Author: Probably not. But I think that writing several poems about characters that all live in one place makes the writing process easier. You don't have to pack all your characters and images into a single poem. The tiger and the cat and the rabbit appear in their own poems elsewhere. My purpose in writing you was simple: I wanted to tell a story. And I have you to thank, my dear poem, for helping me do it.

Nancy Willard

biographical notes

John Agard is a playwright, poet, and children's writer from Guyana, who came to England in 1977. He worked for the Commonwealth Institute from 1978 to 1985, travelling all over the UK as a touring reader, promoting Caribbean culture in schools. He was the first Writer in Residence at the South Bank Centre in London and Poet in Residence at the BBC. He has won several awards for his work, including the Paul Hamlyn Award for Poetry in 1997 and a Cholmondeley Award in 2004. His collection, *We Brits*, was shortlisted for the 2007 British Book Awards Decibel Writer of the Year award. In 2012 he was awarded the Queen's Gold Medal for Poetry. John Agard lives in East Sussex, with his partner, the poet Grace Nichols.

Philip de Vos was a language teacher and afterwards an opera singer and photographer. In 1998 he made a CD in which he sang musical arrangements of his poems. Known in South Africa as a writer of nonsense verse and stories, he has published over 25 books in Afrikaans as well as a book of his photographs and has been awarded several literary prizes for his work. He also published two volumes of verses in English: *Carnival of the Animals* and *Beware of the Canary!* He specialises in rhyming translations, for which he has received two international IBBY awards. He lives in Cape Town.

Carol Ann Duffy, who writes for both children and adults, was born in Glasgow and grew up in England. Since 2009 she has been the UK's Poet Laureate. Her anthology, *Stopping for Death*, won the 2007 Signal Poetry Award and she received an Eric Gregory Award in 1984, a Cholmondeley Award in 1992 and the Dylan Thomas Award from the Poetry Society in 1989. Her collection *Rapture* won the T. S. Eliot Award. In 2012 she was awarded the PEN Pinter Prize in recognition of her outstanding literary merit. Carol Ann Duffy lives in Manchester and is Creative Director of the Writing School at Manchester Metropolitan University.

Jackie Kay was born and brought up in Scotland. Her collection of short stories, *Wish I Was Here*, was published in 2007 to great acclaim. She has won the Guardian Fiction Prize for her novel *Trumpet*, and a Forward Prize for her collection of poetry, *The Adoption Papers*. Jackie Kay lives in Manchester and is Professor Creative Writing at the University of Newcastle.

X. J. Kennedy was born in 1929 in Dover, New Jersey, and at the age of fourteen published a magazine called "Terrifying Test-tube Tales". He attended various universities – Seton Hall, Columbia, the Sorbonne, Michigan – served in the US Navy and taught at various colleges. His collections of poems for adults include *In a Prominent Bar in Secaucus: New and Selected Poems* and *Peeping Tom's Cabin: Comic Verse*. His children's books include collections of verse and two novels, and he has written several textbooks, among them *An Introduction to Poetry* with Dana Gioia, now in its thirteenth edition. In 2009 the Poetry Society of America awarded him the Robert Frost Medal for lifetime service to poetry. X. J. Kennedy and his wife, author Dorothy M. Kennedy, live in Lexington, Massachusetts, where they earn their bread as freelance writers and sometimes read aloud to six grandchildren.

JonArno Lawson was born in Hamilton, Canada. Several of his poetry books for children have been awarded the Lion and Unicorn Award for Excellence in North American Poetry. He also writes for adults. His most recent books are *Enjoy It While It Hurts* and *Footpath Flowers*. JonArno Lawson lives in Toronto with his wife and three children.

Dennis Lee was born in Toronto, Canada, and was the city's first Poet Laureate. He has written more than twenty books for adults and children, as well as the song lyrics for Jim Henson's television series *Fraggle Rock*. His books include *Alligator Pie, Garbage Delight, Jelly Belly, Bubblegum Delicious* and *So Cool*. Dennis Lee lives in Toronto and has three children and two grandsons.

Margaret Mahy is a well-known New Zealand author of

children's and young adult books. Her books, *The Haunting* and *The Changeover*, received the Carnegie Medal. She wrote nearly 50 novels, including *Alchemy* in 2002. Among her children's books, *A Lion in the Meadow* and *The Man Whose Mother was a Pirate* are considered national classics. Her novels have been translated into many different languages. In 2006 she was awarded the Hans Christian Andersen Award (known as the Little Nobel Prize) in recognition of a "lasting contribution to children's literature".

Margaret Mahy lived on Banks Peninsula, Canterbury, in the South Island of New Zealand.

Roger McGough was born in Liverpool, and is the author of over fifty books of poetry for adults and children, and the editor of numerous anthologies. The winner of two BAFTAs and a Royal Television Society award, he also co-wrote the script for the animation of "Yellow Submarine". A Fellow of the Royal Society of Literature, he has a Cholmondeley Award and is a two-time winner of both the Signal and CLPE Awards for the best book of poetry for children. He is an Honorary Professor of Thames Valley University and a Fellow of John Moores University, Liverpool. He was made a Freeman of the City of Liverpool in 2001 and received a CBE from the Queen in 2004 for services to literature. Currently he presents "Poetry Please" on BBC Radio 4. He has four children and lives in Barnes, south-west London.

Adrian Mitchell was born near Hampstead Heath, in London, in 1932 and died in London in 2008. He wrote poems, stories, plays and songs for adults and children. Mitchell's poems for children appear in *Daft as a Doughnut* and *Balloon Lagoon*, both illustrated by Tony Ross. He lived with his wife, Celia, and their golden retriever, Daisy the Dog of Peace, near Hampstead Heath.

Stephen Mitchell's many books include the bestselling *Tao Te Ching: A New English Version*, *Bhagavad Gita: A New Translation*, *Meetings with the Archangel*, *Gilgamesh: A New English Version*, and his translation of the *Iliad*. His books for young readers include *The Wishing Bone*, winner of the 2004 Lee Bennett Hopkins Poetry Award, *Jesus: What He Really Said and Did* and *Genies, Meanies, and Magic Rings*. He lives in California.

Grace Nichols was born in Georgetown, Guyana, in 1950. After working in Guyana as a teacher and journalist, she emigrated to the UK in 1977. Her first collection of poetry, *I Is a Long Memoried Woman* won the 1983 Commonwealth Poetry Prize. She has written several further books of poetry and a novel for adults, *Whole of a Morning Sky*. Her books for children include collections of short stories and poetry anthologies. Her latest work of selected poems is *I Have Crossed an Ocean*. She now lives in East Sussex, with her partner, the poet John Agard.

Naomi Shihab Nye has written or edited more than twenty five books, many for young readers, including *This Same Sky* and *The Space Between Our Footsteps*. She has won many awards for her writing, and was elected Chancellor of the Academy of American Poets in 2010. She lives in San Antonio, Texas.

Jack Prelutsky was born in Brooklyn, New York and is the author of more than fifty poetry collections. For over thirty years, he has been America's most popular children's poet. His award-winning books include *The New Kid on the Block*, *The Dragons Are Singing Tonight* and *If Not for the Cat*. In 2006, the Poetry Foundation named Prelutsky the inaugural winner of the Children's Poet Laureate award. Jack Prelutsky lives in Seattle, Washington.

Anushka Ravishankar has written over fifteen books of verse, fiction and non-fiction, many of which have been published internationally. The majority of these are nonsense or absurd verse, a genre she is particularly fond of. Several of her books have won international awards – *Tiger on a Tree* was given the Star of Excellence by the National Union of Culture and Libraries in France in 1999, and *Anything But a Grabooberry* and *Trash!: On Ragpicker Children and Recycling* received prestigious special mentions in the International White Raven's Catalogue of the World's Best Children's Books in 2000 and 2001 respectively. Apart from children's books, she also writes plays for both children and adults. Anushka Ravishankar lives in Delhi with her family.

Christopher Reid is a British poet, anthologist, publisher and teacher. He has been nominated twice for the Whitbread Awards: in 1996 and 2002. His books of poetry include *Arcadia*, which won the 1980 Somerset Maugham Award and the Hawthornden Prize; *Pea Soup; Katerina Brac; In the Echoey Tunnel; Expanded Universes; For and After* and *Mr Mouth*. He has also written two books of poems for children: *All Sorts*, which won the 2000 Signal Poetry Award, and *Alphabicycle Order*. One of his most recent poetry collections, *A Scattering*, won the 2009 Costa Book of the Year, and was shortlisted for the T. S. Eliot Prize and the Forward Poetry Prize.

Michael Rosen is a children's novelist and poet and the author of 150 books including *You Can't Catch Me*, which won the Signal Poetry Award in 1982, *We're Going on a Bear Hunt*, winner of the Smarties Book Prize in 1990, *The Sad Book*, winner of the Smarties Prize in 2005, and *Alphabet Poem*, which won a WOW award in 2005. Michael Rosen was appointed the UK's fifth Children's Laureate in June 2007, and is Professor in the Department of Education Studies at Goldsmith's, University of London.

Jeanne Steig is the author of several books of light verse and two books of prose, including *Consider the Lemming*, a Parents' Choice Remarkable Book in 1998, *Alpha Beta Chowder, A Handful of Beans*, a New York Times Book Review Best Illustrated Book in 1998, *A Gift from Zeus: Sixteen Favorite Myths*, a Publishers Weekly Best Book of the Year, Smithsonian Magazine's Notable Book of the Year, and a New York Times Notable Book. They were all illustrated by her late husband, William Steig, with the exception of her newest release *Tales From Gizzard's Grill*, which was illustrated by Sandy Turner, and *Fleas!* which was illustrated by Britt Spenser. Her light verse has also been published in the *New Yorker* and in various literary magazines. Jeanne Steig lives in Boston, Massachusetts.

Matthew Sweeney's publications for children include *Up on the Roof: New and Selected Poems* and a novel, *Fox*. He was a resident in Berlin in 2005-2006 as a guest of The German Academic Exchange Service DAAD, under their Invited Artists programme. His most recent books of poems are *The Night Post* and *Black Moon*, which was shortlisted for the T. S. Eliot Prize. He is the co-author of *Writing Poetry* and the editor of several anthologies.

Richard Wilbur's poems have won various awards, including two Pulitzers, and have been gathered in *Collected Poems 1943-2004*, which includes his children's verse as well. His translations of Molière and Racine are widely performed, and his rendering of Corneille's baroque masterpiece *The Theatre of Illusion (L'Illusion Comique)* won him a National Translation Award in 2010. Richard Wilbur lives in Cummington, Massachusetts.

Nancy Willard is the author of two novels, twelve books of poetry and numerous books for children. She has edited one anthology of poems for young people, *Step Lightly: Poems for the Journey. A Visit to William Blake's Inn: Poems for Innocent and Experienced Travellers* was the first poetry book to win the Newbery Medal. Her most recent book for children *A Starlit Snowfall* was published in 2011. She teaches in the English Department at Vassar College, New York State.

acknowledgements

The editor and publisher gratefully acknowledge permission to use the following material:

"Old World New World" © John Agard from *Under the Moon & Over the Sea* edited by John Agard and Grace Nichols, published by Walker Books, 2002, used with permission of Caroline Sheldon Literary Agency; "Five Girls" © Carol Ann Duffy from *Meeting Midnight*, published by Faber and Faber Ltd, 1999; "Aquarium" © Philip de Vos from *Carnival of the Animals*, published by Human and Rousseau, 1998; "The Stincher" © Jackie Kay from *Three Has Gone*, published by Blackie Children's Books, 1994, used with permission of PFD; "The Octopus and the Seahorse" © JonArno Lawson from *The Man in the Moon-Fixer's Mask*, published by Pedlar Press, 2004; "Alligator Pie" © Dennis Lee, published by Key Porter Books 1974; "The Man from the Land of Fandango" © Margaret Mahy from *Nonstop Nonsense*, published by Margaret K. McElderry Books, 1989, used with permission of Watson Little Ltd; "Didgeridoo" © Roger McGough from *All the Best: The Selected Poems of Roger McGough*, published by Puffin Books, 2004, used with permission of PFD; "Riding West from Little Bear" © Adrian Mitchell from *Daft as a Doughnut*, published by Orchard Books, 2004; "The Wishing Bone" © Stephen Mitchell, published by Candlewick Press, 2003; "Sun is Laughing" © Grace Nichols from *A Caribbean Dozen: Poems from Caribbean Poets* edited by Grace Nichols and John Agard, published by Walker Books, 1994; "Supple Cord" © Naomi Shihab Nye from *A Maze Me: Poems for Girls*, published by Greenwillow Books, 2005; "The Kraken" © Jack Prelutsky from *The Headless Horseman Rides Tonight*, published by Greenwillow Books, 1980; Excerpt from "Excuse Me, Is This India?" © Anushka Ravishankar, excerpted from the book *Excuse Me, Is this India?*, first published by Tara Publishing © 2001; "Skip Don't Trip" © Christopher Reid from *All Sorts*, published by Ondt and Gracehoper, 1999, used with permission of Ondt & Gracehoper; "Thirty-Two Laps" © Michael Rosen from *Quick! Let's Get Out of Here*, published by Andre Deutsch, 1983, used with permission of PFD; "Bellicose Brigand vs Belligerent Bear" © Jeanne Steig from *Alpha Beta Chowder*, published by HarperCollins Publishers, 1992, used with permission of Pippin Properties, Inc; "Cows On The

Beach" © Matthew Sweeney from *The Flying Spring Onion*, published by Faber and Faber, 1992; excerpt from "The Disappearing Alphabet" © Richard Wilbur from *The Disappearing Alphabet*, published by Harcourt Children's Books, 2001; "Blake Leads a Walk on the Milky Way" © Nancy Willard from *A Visit to William Blake's Inn: Poems for Innocent and Experienced Travellers*, published by Harcourt Children's Books, 1981.

Every reasonable effort has been made to trace ownership of and/or secure permission for the use of copyrighted material. If notified of any omission, the editors and publisher will gladly make the necessary correction in future printings.

I would like to thank:
Caroline Royds, my editor at Walker Books,
whose idea this was, who made many helpful suggestions,
and who made the whole experience a great deal of fun,
her hard-working and helpful assistant, Genevieve Herr
and the designer Beth Aves;
my wife Amy, and my children, Sophie, Asher
and Joseph, for their support and always helpful input.
Lissa Paul who, through her books and conversation,
introduced me to the work of many of the poets included here,
and Michael Joseph for our essential and
stimulating e-mail correspondence;
Bill Condon, Reviva Schermbrucker, Karabo Kgoleng,
Richard Flynn, Joseph T. Thomas Jr.
(Thomas's book *Poetry's Playground* should be read
by anyone interested in children's poetry),
Bob Barton, Nancy Chambers, Anne Harvey, June Factor,
Celia Jellett, Maureen Nimon, Sara Fanelli,
Lena Coakley at CANSCAIP, Peter Carver,
R. P. MacIntyre, John Foster, and Ms. Glendy Lee
(Children's Librarian at the Hong Kong Public Library),
for help with my research.
Finally, thank you to Claas Kazzer, whose website for the
Signal Poetry Award also brought many fine poets
and books to my attention.

JonArno Lawson

If you enjoyed this Walker poetry book,
why not take a look at these!

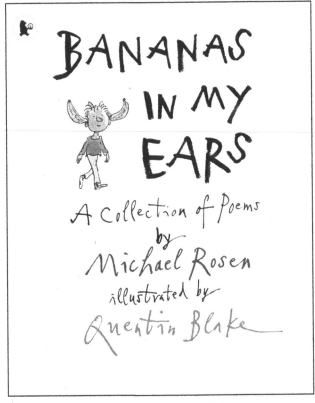

BANANAS IN MY EARS

A Collection of Poems
by
Michael Rosen
illustrated by
Quentin Blake

ISBN 978-1-4063-3755-6

ISBN 978-1-4063-1208-9

ISBN 978-1-4063-1701-5

ISBN 978-1-4063-0888-4

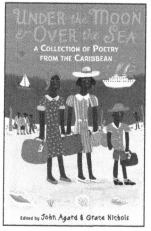

ISBN 978-1-4063-3448-7

Available at all good booksellers
www.walker.co.uk